MATH 001

In the Beginning

Maritime Anthropology (MATH) a topic which covers prehistoric, historic and modern life, and inspirations derived from the world's oceans and the brave souls who have subsisted on and inhabited the surrounding environs of the sea.

MATH 001 In the Beginning specifically focuses on the ancient myths, and ancient people who explored the world's oceans and developed maritime culture as it is currently known.

Research and module development

by

Yvonne-Cher Skye

Skye Research

Statement of Purpose

To create an educational program from which educators can create a program to sell to potential students as part of a maritime cultural experience. The intended audience can be variable from a one hour, one day seminar course to an 18 week course semester.

The actual lesson plans are at the discretion of the instructor. The materials available in this booklet are meant to be a reference point to assist the instructor in developing a foundation from which the intended course can be derived.

As this is in the early stages of production, all comments and suggestions for improvement are welcome.

Sincerely,

Yvonne-Cher Skye

Table of Contents

Summary

Objective:

Lecture on the topics of early maritime history in ancient and prehistoric times.

Materials Needed:

Instructor: PowerPoint Presentation

Students: Journals, writing implements

Vocabulary introduced:

- Amphitrite

- Aphrodite

- Archetype

- Castor and Pollux

- Great floods

- Hero and Leander

- King Neptune

- Manannan Celtic Sea God

- Maui, Creator of New Zealand

- Moses and the Red Sea

- Nereus

- Oceanus

- Oceanids

- Portunus

- Poseidon

- Rainbow

Background:

All of Maritime History began with the observation of the oceans and rivers by man. The process of naming of deities to describe what was observed is a universal archetype in which this course will entertain and educate the students as to the various attributes that are assigned to each deity and maritime event.

Further specific lectures can be assigned module letters as the need arises.

Reference:

Seafaring Lore and Legend, Peter D. Jeans 2007
Wikipedia

Lesson Plan:

Introduce the terms and concepts via PowerPoint by using images and bulleted lists to convey the information. Dialogue with the students in a question and answer format.

Introduction:

Explain mythological archetypes in the context of maritime lore. Using specific examples such as God of the Sea, Wife of the God of the Sea, Monsters, Curses, describing natural phenomenon, creation myths, and others.

Body:

- Amphitrite - list attributes

- Aphrodite - list attributes

- Castor and Pollux - list attributes

- Great floods - list attributes

- Hero and Leander - list attributes

- King Neptune - list attributes

- Manannan Celtic Sea God - list attributes

- Maui, Creator of New Zealand - list attributes

- Moses and the Red Sea - list attributes

- Nereus - list attributes

- Oceanus - list attributes

- Portunus - list attributes

- Poseidon - list attributes

- Rainbow - list attributes

Conclusion:
Question and answer session to review materials.

Clean-Up:
Students take their things with them.

Learning sessions

Textbook reading chapters can be developed per the Instructor's chosen textbook or via their own manual dependent on scope of material intended to be covered in this course

Individual sections with dividers each focusing on one component of the content: All of the following will be determined by Instructor, module course outline gives examples of the following:

    a. Learning outcomes

    b. Session Information

    c. Learning activities

    d. Learning Resources

    e. Evaluation Procedures

    f. Timing and assignment

Course Outline

Catalog number: MATH 001　　　　　　**Course Title:** In the Beginning

Year: 2017　　　　　　　　　　　　　　**Semester:** Spring

Instructor:　　　　　　　　　　　　　**Office Location:**

Office Hours:

Objectives of the course:

Explain mythological archetypes in the context of maritime lore.

Understand ancient maritime history.

Understand the lifeways and mindset of ancient maritime people.

Any measurable objectives that can be demonstrated by student.

Procedures for accomplishing these objectives:

Lectures

Class discussions

Analytic questions

Projects

Research papers

Use of visual and oral reports

Fields trips

Visiting lecturers

Student testimonials

Use of multimedia i.e. videos, audio recordings to exemplify topics

Student requirements for completion of the course:

Varies per instructor discretion and length of program

During introductory lecture, the instructor must list specific work students must complete in order to receive credit for the course

Student need to demonstrate the accomplishment of each objective, examples are as follows:

Read all the chapters in the textbook

Submit a research paper

Oral report on topic

Submit book report

Complete lab reports

Complete periodic quizzes

Complete mid-term exam

Complete final exam

Grading Practices:

Students will be graded using above methods, at the instructor's discretion

Relative importance of each item

Four quizzes: 40%

Two book reports 20%

Term paper 20%

Final exam 20%

Equals 100%

Rules Concerning student absence and lateness:

At the discretion of the instructor and student agreement

If marina, ship or school follows specific rules, then state explicitly

Textbook:

List author, title publisher, date of publication of any required texts, manuals

Weekly Outline Topics to be covered:

List topics in sequential order, examples included with this packet are:

Great Floods

Moses and the Red Sea

The Rainbow

Maui, creator of New Zealand

Oceanus

King Neptune

Poseidon

Amphritrite

Aphrodite

Portunus

Castor and Pollux

Nereus

Hero and Lander

Mannan, Celtic Sea God

List tests, quizzes, due dates for papers

Audio Visual Materials to be used:

List any visual elements to be used during course including:

PowerPoint presentations

Youtube videos

Photos

Graphs

Maps

List of supplementary readings:

MATH 001 Glossary

List books, periodicals, articles which students should read in addition to tex

Miscellaneous information:

Any information that will further clarify what is hoped to be achieved in the course and how you plan to achieve it.

Audio Visual Experience

Photos

Please see attached document entitled Photos.

These will be updated as research is continued.

Useful weblinks leading to images can be found on the following websites:

Websites on subject

http://www.merriam-webster.com/dictionary/archetype

https://skyeresearchygfi.wordpress.com/2016/06/09/math-marine-anthropology-001-summary/

https://skyeresearchygfi.wordpress.com/2016/09/03/math-001-youtube-channel/

Audio recordings, videos or script to explain each section

Youtube channel Playlist MATH 001 at this link:

https://www.youtube.com/playlist?

list=PLBHbcZSn310CUhmMTkHoPqJlylPpYw1Jr

Appendices

Glossary

Maps

Artistic renderings

Works Cited

Glossary

A

Adonis – Mortal lover of Aphrodite.

Aeneas – in Greek Mythology the child of Aphrodite.

Amphitrite – Is a Goddess in Greek mythology. She is the queen of the sea. She is the wife of Poseidon.

Anchises – Mortal lover of Aphrodite, he was a Trojan.

Anteros – in Greek Mythology the child of Aphrodite.

Aphrodite – Is a Goddess in Greek mythology. She is the wife of Hephaestus. She is the Goddess of love, beauty and sexual rapture. Born of the sea foam she is a patron of Sailors. Daughter of Zeus and Dione.

Aphros – sea foam

Archetype – Is a psychological term which defines the original pattern or model of which all things of the same type are representations or copies, often describes themes within stories, myths and fables.

Ashtart – is a goddess in Syro-Palestinian Mythology who is the counterpart of Aphrodite.

C

Castor and Pollux – Are characters in Greek and Roman mythology. They are twin brothers. They are believed to be of the Gemini constellation. They are the patron gods of shipwrecked sailors and brings favorable wind for those who made sacrifices to them.

Cronus – castrated his Father and of the Gods in Greek Mythology. Cronus who tossed the genitals into the sea which began to churn and foam which formed Aphrodite.

Cupid – is a God in Roman Mythology who is the son of Venus.

Deluge – Is a climatic event that results from a tremendous release of waters, typically from clouds which results in floods, and related geological events such as mudslides.

Dione – Mother of Aphrodite, and consort of Zeus in Greek Mythology.

Doris – is a goddess in Greek Mythology. Mother of Amphitrite. She is the wife of Nereus.

Eros – he is a God in Greek Mythology. He is the child of Aphrodite.

Flood – same as a deluge, further defined as a hydroclimatic extreme of excessive moisture within the atmosphere and environment.

G

Gilgamesh – a hero of Babylonian Mythology.

Graces– are goddesses in Greek Mythology, who accompany Aphrodite.

H

Hades – is the realm of the dead, in the underworld.

Helen – In Greek Mythology, the sister of Castor and Pollux and the reason for the Trojan War.

Hephaestus – In Greek Mythology, is the steadiest of the gods, and husband of Aphrodite.

Hero and Leander – Are characters from Greek Mythology. They are famous lovers who participated in a forbidden affair. Leander was the man, while Hero was the woman. They drowned and became patrons of sailors as a result.

I

Ishtar – is a goddess in Mesopotamian Mythology, who is the counterpart to Aphrodite.

J

Jason and the Argonauts - iOn their voyage to search for the Golden Fleece, Pollux shows his boxing skills by killing the King of the Bebryces.

L

Leda - is the Mother of Castor and Pollux, in Greek Mythology. Castor sired by Tyndareus, and Pollus was sired by Zeus. Queen of Sparta.

M

Manannan – A god in Celtic mythology. He is the Sea God, and offerings were made to appease him when embarking upon a seagoing voyage.

Maui – Is a demi-god of the Polynesian Islands. His name means No ordinary man. Using a hook, he fished up the island of New Zealand. Thus, he is credited with creating New Zealand.

Moses – Is a character in Judeo-Christian mythology. He is of the Hero archetype. One of his stories, consists of crossing the Red Sea via a miracle and communication with his god to cause the miracle.

N

Neptune, King – Is a god in Roman mythology. He is the patron god of freshwater and the sea. His daughters are of patrons of the rivers, and lakes. He is also the patron of horse racing.

Nereus – Is a God in Greek mythology. He is the God of the Sea.

O

Oceanus – Is a God in Greek mythology. He was a Titan. He is the father of the river gods and Oceanids.

Orpheus – was a sailor with Jason and the Argonauts, he played his harp to appease the Gods.

P

Polydeuces – In Greek Mythology refers to twins.

Portunus – Is a God in Roman mythology. He is the God of rivers, harbors, gates, and portals. He is depicted with a key and sometimes an anchor

Poseidon – Is a God in Greek mythology. He is the protector of all waters. He is always depicted with a Triton.

Prototype – A perfect example; an inherited idea or mode of thought in the psychology of C. G. Jung that is derived from the experience of the race and is present in the unconscious of the individual

S

Salacia – Is a the Roman Goddess equivalent of Amphitrite The third one who encircles the sea.

T

Tethys – Mother of Amphitrite A goddess of Greek Mythology. She is the wife of Oceanus.

Triton – is a fishman, he is the son of Amphitrite

Tuatha De Danann – Are a group of deities and nature spirits who held council over all life in ancient Celtic myth.

Tyndareus – King of Sparta and father of Castor of the Greek Twins Castor and Pollux.

U

Uranus – Father of the Gods in Greek Mythology. Castrated by his son Cronus who tossed the genitals into the sea which began to churn and foam which formed Aphrodite.

Utrapishtim – an old storyteller in Babylonian Mythology.

Venus ~ is a Goddess in Roman Mythology who is the counterpart to Aphrodite.

Maps

will be added per the request and special requirements of the instructor.

Artistic renderings

will be added per the request and special requirements of the instructor.

Works Cited

http://www.merriam-webster.com/dictionary

Back Page

For further sources and information on the research conducted on this topic, it is recommended that you order the supplemental materials entitled notes and photos.